6/93

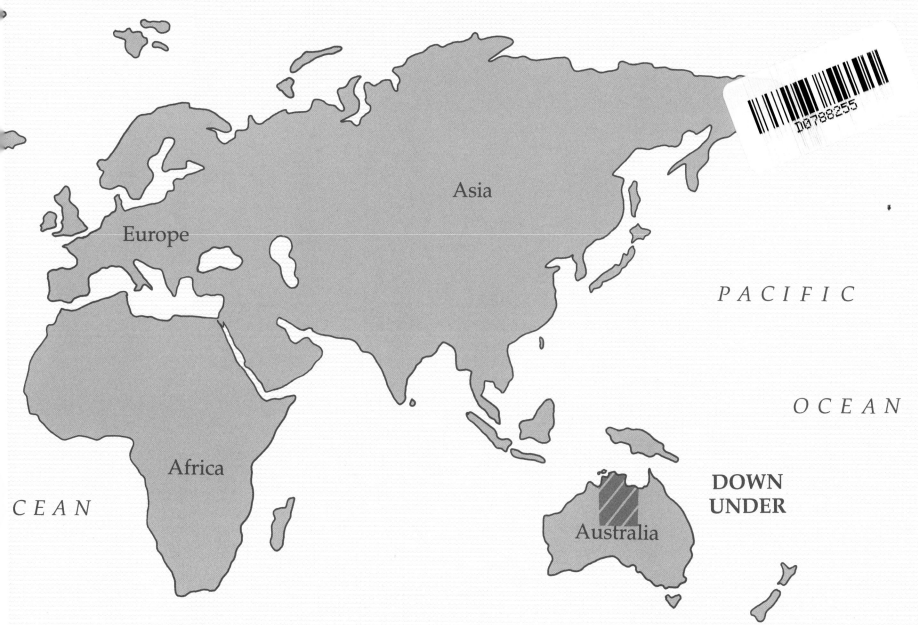

Europe

Asia

PACIFIC

OCEAN

Africa

CEAN

DOWN
UNDER

Australia

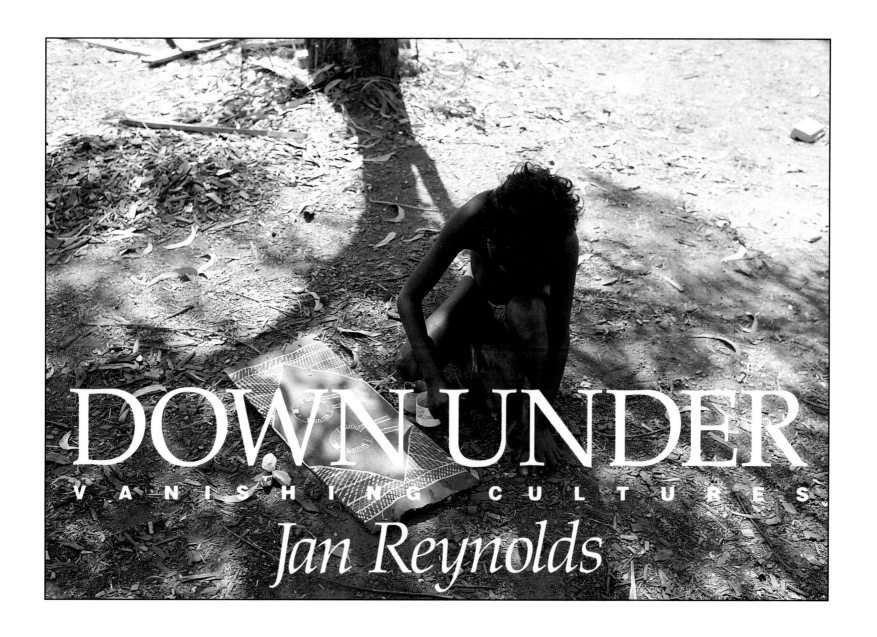

DOWN UNDER
VANISHING CULTURES
Jan Reynolds

Harcourt Brace Jovanovich, Publishers
San Diego   New York   London

HBJ

Requests for permission to make copies of any part
of the work should be mailed to: Permissions Department,
Harcourt Brace Jovanovich, Publishers, 8th Floor, Orlando, Florida 32887.

Library of Congress Cataloging-in-Publication Data
Reynolds, Jan. 1956–
Down under: vanishing cultures / text and photographs
by Jan Reynolds. — 1st ed.
p.   cm.
Summary: Examines the vanishing culture of the Tiwi tribe,
aborigines who live on a small island off the coast of Australia.
ISBN 0-15-224182-5   ISBN 0-15-224183-3 (pbk.)
1. Tiwi (Australian people) — Juvenile literature. [1. Tiwi
(Australian people) 2. Australian aborigines.] I. Title.
DU125.T5R48   1992
994'.8 — dc20   91-9791

First edition
A B C D E   A B C D E (pbk.)

To my six siblings, and
all caring brothers and sisters
around the world
— J. R.

Photographic work supported by the
Professional Photography Division of Eastman Kodak Co.

To take the photographs in this book, the author used two
35mm Nikon cameras with 20mm, 35mm, 105mm, and 180mm lenses.
The display and text type were set in Palatino
by Thompson Type, San Diego, California.
Color separations were made by Bright Arts, Ltd., Singapore.
Printed and bound by Tien Wah Press, Singapore
Production supervision by Warren Wallerstein and Ginger Boyer
Designed by Camilla Filancia

INTRODUCTION

The Tiwi are aborigines who live on a small island just off the coast of Australia. For shelter, they make simple roofs out of tree bark, and sometimes they sleep out under the open sky. On walkabout, the Tiwi travel through the bush, or wild country, moving from place to place where they know they will find water and food. They believe the landscape was shaped long ago during the Dreamtime, and while on walkabout, they can return to this time. For the aborigines, the natural landscape has its own beautiful spirit that will never change, and in the Dreamtime, they share this spirit with the land.

But the aborigines' ancient way of life is disappearing. New roads and towns change the shape and natural rhythm of the landscape and interfere with the traditional pathways of walkabout.

We and the aborigines are all part of the same human family, and the loss of the Tiwi's traditional way of life is our loss, too. Like the aborigines, we all depend on the natural world to live. We all share this earth, its lands and waters. And because of this, perhaps we should take a look at the aborigines' life in harmony with nature before it vanishes forever.

Far down under, the bright sun sets over one of Australia's tiny islands.

Inside a ring of small fires that keep wild animals away at night, a young aboriginal girl named Amprenula whispers to her mother, asking for one more story. She curls up close as her mother begins her tale about their tribe, the Tiwi.

"Long ago, your great-grandmother went on walkabout, walking day after day across the land, searching for food and fresh water. When she traveled the same path many times, she entered the Dreamtime. Aborigines believe in the Dreamtime, the time when our great ancestors, the Sky Heroes, shaped the land and created everything on earth . . . including us.

"Just like Great-grandmother, when we go on walkabout, we become part of the land, part of the Dreamtime. This land we live on is very special. It belongs to no one person. It is here for all of us.

"This is why your great-grandfather taught you to dance your own Dreaming, the dance you were given when you were born.

*Amprenula dancing her Dreaming
with her little cousin*

"When you dance, you also become part of the land."

Rock art

Soon Amprenula sleeps and dances in her dreams.

The next day, Amprenula's mother shows her how to collect string bark. These strips of bark are used to build simple roofs for shade from the hot afternoon sun. They can also be woven to make the baskets that the Tiwi carry when they go on walk-about. The Tiwi paint their baskets with bright designs.

On walkabout, aborigines follow the same paths their ancestors traveled long ago. They carry few things with them, and they look for food as they move from place to place.

Using a small mirror, Amprenula reflects light into a hollow log, and she sees something move. Grandmother chops at the log, hoping to scare the animal out.

She chops halfway through, but nothing happens. So she uses a long stick to push inside the log . . . and out runs a small bandicoot. Amprenula quickly captures it.

Inside another log, Tipalipimuri, Grandmother's adopted son, has found a large carpet snake. The snake cannot be scared out like the bandicoot, so they chop a hole in the log to pull the snake through.

The Tiwi always get their food from the land just as their ancestors did. Tipalipimuri helps Grandmother look for other things to eat as they continue on their journey.

After walking many hours, it is time to stop and rest. When the snake and bandicoot are cooked, Amprenula's mother also bakes bread in the hot ashes for everyone to eat.

Her family is thirsty, so Amprenula goes to a spring to fetch water. On her way, she almost falls into a large hole dug by a boar, a wild pig the Tiwi also hunt to eat.

The water Amprenula collects is cold and clear because it comes from deep in the ground.

Early the next morning, Grandmother lights a fire to burn away some of the thick, dead grasses that cover the ground. This helps both the Tiwi and the animals. Fire burns away the brush, making it easier for the Tiwi to travel. And new green plants will grow in the cleared area, providing fresh food for the animals. The fire will not spread far because it will burn itself out.

While the fire is burning, Amprenula and Tipalipimuri go for *malaki*, a bath, in the small river nearby.

When the fire is out, they follow the small river to the coast. Here, where the fresh water flows into the ocean, the river turns into a mangrove swamp. When the tide flows out, the long roots of the mangrove trees are uncovered. Among this tangle of roots and mud, the Tiwi find crabs, mussels, and other shellfish to eat.

As a treat, Amprenula and her mother also look for mangrove worms that live in the thick juice under the bark of the tree. They like to eat these worms fresh, the moment they find them.

Hungry crocodiles sometimes swim in the waters that flow out to the ocean from the mangrove swamp. Amprenula, Tipalipimuri, and their small cousin like to swim in these waters, too. But they always take care to watch for crocodiles.

The beach at the edge of the mangrove swamp can be a fun place to play. Especially when friends from other Tiwi families show up to run and splash in the water together.

After playing on the beach, Amprenula and Tipalipimuri continue to look for food for their family and relatives. Amprenula goes off to dig in the sand for turtle eggs. Tipalipimuri goes spearfishing in the shallow waters with some friends.

Tiwi spirit poles

Family and relatives are very important to the aborigines. The Tiwi even cut and carve beautiful poles from trees to honor relatives who have died. These spirit poles are painted with natural dyes that were baked in a fire before being used.

On this walkabout, Amprenula's family has made a spirit pole for one of their relatives. Some family members paint their faces and bodies for the ceremony that follows the placing of the pole in the ground.

When the ceremony begins, a fire is built. Family members walk around and through the smoke to send their relative's spirit on its way to the spirit world. Then they dance their Dreamings around the spirit pole to honor the relative they have lost.

Spirit pole made by Amprenula's family

Relatives dancing their Dreamings

Amprenula lives in a land where her ancestors have lived for thousands of years. When she goes on walkabout or dances her Dreaming, she becomes part of the Dreamtime — part of the land. She is proud to be an aborigine living with her family in the bush.

Amprenula leaning against an anthill

There were only four of us: two other women—Timira-matu and Chiplet—little Amprenula, and me. The fires we had lit had died out, except for the one glowing slightly near where I lay on the ground. Whether by instinct or a subtle sound, I don't know . . . but I woke to two eyes reflecting a deep red color in the low light of the coals. I sat up with a start and called to the other women, but the eyes had already disappeared into the bush. The two women fanned the dying embers encircling our camp, adding dry grasses that made the flames shoot up. Little Amprenula huddled in the dark, her senses heightened by excitement. We were on walkabout, and nocturnal visits by wild animals aren't unusual out in the Australian bush.

Timiramatu, Chiplet, Amprenula, and the group of aborigines I was with are Tiwi, who live on Bathurst Island just off the top end of the Northern Territories. Their ancestors have been living there for somewhere in the vicinity of fifty thousand years. How the aborigines came to Australia isn't actually known. Some anthropologists believe the aborigines' ancestors came across a land bridge that is now gone, and some believe they came by boat from Asia. But the aborigines say their ancestors came to be here because of a Great Spirit from an island far across the sea, where their own spirits return when they die.

With our circle of fire keeping the wild animals at bay, I felt safe and secure . . . a strange, deeply primitive sense. The evening was so warm, we simply lay together under a blanket of bright, thick stars surrounding the Southern Cross. Timiramatu had taken me into her extended family to go on walkabout—a spiritual journey and continuous search for food in remote country—in an area she had known all her sixty-some-odd years. We traveled light to cover ground more easily. These days, an ax, a bucket, and, occasionally, a rifle are taken along, but not so many years ago people took only string-bark baskets, handcrafted tools, and fired ironwood spears.

We spent many days traveling together. One day I heard the crackling of fire directly behind me; Timiramatu's adopted son, Tipalipimuri, had lit flames that spread quickly in the dry bush. I remembered that just that morning, Timiramatu had shown me a plant that, once lit, can smolder for days, ready for immediate use. The Tiwi carry it with them, never letting it go out. Tipalipimuri had used this plant to light the bush fire. Apparently, after the heavy rains of the wet season stop and the grasses become brittle in the dry season, the aborigines burn the thick areas. This makes traveling easier, and after the fire has burned itself out, new green shoots soon begin to grow, attracting animals. Since we were on our way to a freshwater stream, our destination was safe enough from the blaze.

We also spent days wading in mangrove swamps. Timiramatu told me how the Tiwi collect sticks and pile them on the shores, and when the moon is high and bright, they hunt ducks at night with these throwing sticks.

As we gathered periwinkles, mussels, crabs, and mangrove worms, we constantly combed the shores for the telltale eyes of a crocodile. These creatures can live to be one hundred years old, grow to be thirty feet long, and they don't need to be hungry to eat—if something moves, they snap. But Amprenula and Tipalipimuri weren't afraid; they had an uncanny awareness of all that was happening around them. However, I was feeling vulnerable, very much a part of the food chain.

Beyond the need for hunting and gathering food, going on walkabout has a spiritual meaning. When the aborigine is on walkabout, the land reflects a sacred geography, and the trip becomes a Dream Journey, connecting the travelers to the Dreamtime, the time when the world was created. During the Dreamtime, the Sky Heroes created the earth and its creatures, then, upon completion, became features of the landscape themselves. Consequently, the land is a sacred dimension in aboriginal life.

To get a spiritual message, the people regularly traverse tribal territory on sacred pathways. Because the aborigines have no written language, these pathways are passed down from one generation to the next in songs, called songlines. While on walkabout or a Dream Journey, the aborigine is connected to the eternal moment of creation in the present, which is more a state of mind than any particular place. The Dream Journey is the aboriginal path to spiritual renewal because the people and the land are inseparable.

While on walkabout, word had spread that there was to be a ceremony for an elderly woman in Timaramatu's family who had passed away a couple of months ago. After death, time is left for the spirit to be in contact with family and friends, then it is released and sent on to the spirit world. In preparation for the ceremony, Timiramatu and some of the other elders painted themselves. When aborigines are decorated, they believe they become Sky Heroes as they dance their Dreamings. The Dreaming dances represent things such as Fast Wind or Crocodile and are given to children at birth by their grandfathers. While dancing their Dreamings, aborigines spiritually connect themselves to the land and to the Dreamtime. The drumming of feet during the dance draws the earth into dialogue with the dancers, allowing the ceremony to bring the power of the Dreaming to life.

A smoky fire was built, and people gathered and moved around it, issuing a farewell. Articles owned by the deceased were hung on a line supported by a funeral pole unique to the Tiwi. These poles are works of art, carved and then painted with natural dyes. They are left standing in the ground to honor the deceased.

A sense of awe ran through me as I watched and participated in the ceremony. After living with Timiramatu and her family, sharing their intimate beliefs day by day, I was left with a strong feeling for the earth as one vast network of relationships. I began to see that, like the aborigines, all people are inseparable from the land. And when the last traditional aborigine is gone, it means more than a disappearance of a way of life: it's the loss of humankind in deep harmony with nature, at peace with their world.

—Jan Reynolds

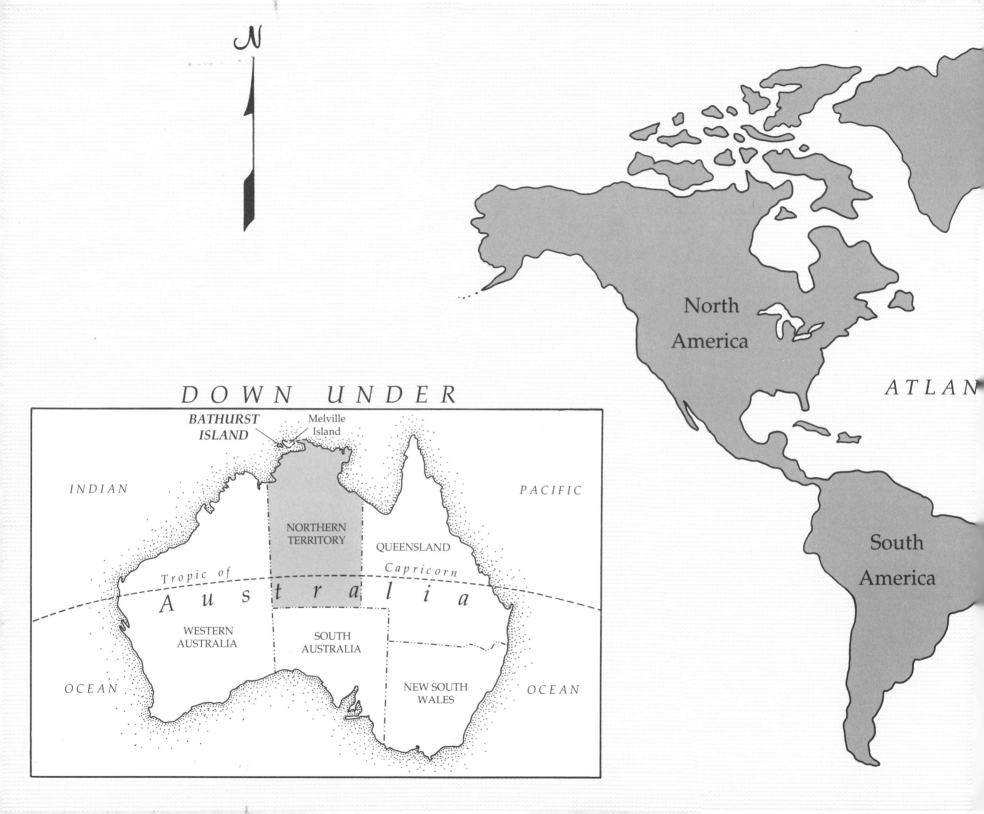

N

DOWN UNDER

BATHURST ISLAND
Melville Island

INDIAN

PACIFIC

NORTHERN TERRITORY

QUEENSLAND

Tropic of

Capricorn

A u *s* t *r* a *l* i *a*

WESTERN AUSTRALIA

SOUTH AUSTRALIA

NEW SOUTH WALES

OCEAN

OCEAN

North
America

ATLAN

South
America